BELARUS: HUMAN RIGHTS

EXECUTIVE SUMMARY

Belarus is an authoritarian state. The country's constitution provides for a directly elected president, who is head of state, and a bicameral parliament, the national assembly. A prime minister appointed by the president is the nominal head of government, but power is concentrated in the presidency, both de jure and de facto. Since his election as president in 1994, Alyaksandr Lukashenka has consolidated his rule over all institutions and undermined the rule of law through authoritarian means, including manipulated elections and arbitrary decrees. All subsequent presidential elections, including the one held in 2010, were neither free nor fair and fell well short of international standards. The September 2012 parliamentary elections also failed to meet international standards. Civilian authorities, Lukashenka in particular, maintained effective control over the security forces. Security forces committed human rights abuses.

The most significant human rights problems continued to be: citizens were unable to change their government through elections; in a system bereft of checks and balances, authorities committed frequent, serious abuses; and persons remained imprisoned on politically motivated charges, while the government failed to account for longstanding cases of politically motivated disappearances.

Other human rights problems included abuses by security forces, which beat detainees and protesters and reportedly used torture or mistreatment during investigations and in prisons. Prison conditions remained extremely poor. Authorities arbitrarily arrested, detained, and imprisoned citizens for criticizing officials, participating in demonstrations, and other political reasons. The judiciary suffered from a lack of independence and political interference; trial outcomes often appeared predetermined, and trials frequently were conducted behind closed doors or in absentia. Authorities continued to infringe on the right of privacy. The government restricted civil liberties, including freedom of speech, press, assembly, association, religion, and movement. The government seized printed materials from civil society activists and prevented independent media from disseminating information and materials. The government continued to hinder or prevent the activities of some religious groups, at times fining them or restricting their services. Official corruption in all branches of government remained a problem. Authorities harassed human rights groups, nongovernmental organizations (NGOs), and political parties, refusing to register many and then threatening them with criminal prosecution for operating without registration. Violence and discrimination against women were problems, as was violence against children. Trafficking in persons remained a significant problem. There was discrimination against lesbian, gay, bisexual, and transgender (LGBT) persons, persons with disabilities, Roma, ethnic minorities, persons with HIV/AIDS, and those who sought to use the Belarusian language. Authorities harassed and at times dismissed members of independent unions from employment in state-owned enterprises, severely limiting the ability of workers to form and join independent trade unions and to organize and bargain collectively.

Authorities at all levels operated with impunity and failed to take steps to prosecute or punish officials in the government or security forces who committed human rights abuses.

Section 1. Respect for the Integrity of the Person, Including Freedom from:

a. Arbitrary or Unlawful Deprivation of Life

During the year there were no reports that the government or its agents committed arbitrary or unlawful killings. The Investigations Committee examines killings and other abuses committed by security forces.

b. Disappearance

There were no developments in the reportedly continuing investigations into the 2000 disappearance of journalist Zmitser Zavadski and the 1999 disappearances of former deputy prime minister Viktar Hanchar, former interior minister Yury Zakharanka, and businessman Anatol Krasouski. There was evidence of government involvement in the disappearances, but authorities continued to deny any connection with them. Following earlier practice, the Investigations Committee again extended the 13-year investigation into the disappearance of Zakharanka at least twice during the year. Human rights advocates argued that the law does not criminalize enforced disappearances by state agents or by those acting with the authorization, support, or acquiescence of the state. Also, human rights activists urged the government against ending investigations of disappearances when the statute of limitations expires in 2014 for the 1999 disappearances.

c. Torture and Other Cruel, Inhuman, or Degrading Treatment or Punishment

The law prohibits such practices. Nevertheless, the Committee for State Security (KGB), riot police, and other security forces, often unidentified and in plain clothes, continued to beat detainees and demonstrators routinely. Security forces also reportedly used torture during investigations. During arrests police frequently beat criminal suspects and persons detained for organizing or participating in demonstrations and other opposition activities, as well as common citizens. For example, on July 7, police officers violently arrested and mistreated at least four elderly persons for reportedly trading without a permit at a market in Pinsk. The chief of the regional police apologized to the public on July 16, acknowledging that the officers' conduct was "unprofessional."

On July 10, a Minsk district court denied an appeal filed by Uladzimir Nyaklyaeu, former presidential candidate and political prisoner, against the city prosecutor's office for refusing to open criminal proceedings regarding his beating on election day in December 2010. At the court hearing, a representative of the prosecutor's office claimed that neither Interior Ministry officers nor KGB special-task units engaged in any operations against Nyaklyaeu. Before the polls closed, police stopped a group of supporters led by Nyaklyaeu and a van carrying a sound system for the demonstration. A group of unidentified men in black uniforms believed to be special forces tossed stun grenades at the group. They beat Nyaklyaeu in the attack and seized the sound equipment. Supporters took him to a hospital for treatment, but unidentified men later abducted him from his hospital bed and held him at the KGB detention center.

Human rights advocates, opposition leaders, and activists released from detention facilities continued to report torture and other forms of physical and psychological abuse of suspects during criminal and administrative investigations.

Despite numerous complaints and appeals to courts and prosecutors, the Investigations Committee refused to re-open a criminal case involving the beatings of a parking lot watchman, Vasil Sarochyk, who police allegedly abused in November 2012. Two police officers detained Sarochyk and transported him to a district office where he was handcuffed and beaten by officers for six hours. The police officers attempted to force Sarochyk to give self-incriminating testimony that he had stolen tombstones stored at the parking lot as well as diesel fuel and car batteries. According to Sarochyk, police hit him with batons on his head and body and threatened to kill him. He complained to prosecutors and in December 2012 investigators announced that four police officers were suspects in the case and accused of abusing authority. In late December 2012, however, all charges were dismissed, and the case was unexpectedly closed. On January 15, Lukashenka denied the torture allegations against the police and said that he "lost interest" in the case when he heard that "it was a woman [officer] beating up a man." In March prosecutors reported that they were studying the case and allowed Sarochyk and his lawyer to access case materials. No new charges were brought against police officers before year's end.

Some hazing of new army recruits, including beatings and other forms of physical and psychological abuse, reportedly continued, although less so than in previous years due to the government's increased prosecution of offenders. In 2011 the Prosecutor General's Office stated that military leaders and prosecutors were taking "effective measures" to prevent deaths, injuries, and incidents of hazing in the army.

Prison and Detention Center Conditions

Prison and detention center conditions remained poor and in many cases posed threats to life and health.

Physical Conditions: According to local activists and human rights lawyers, there were shortages of food, medicine, warm clothing, and bedding as well as inadequate access to basic or emergency medical care and clean drinking water. Ventilation in cells and overall sanitation were poor, and authorities failed to provide conditions necessary for maintaining proper personal hygiene. Prisoners frequently complained of malnutrition and low-quality uniforms and bedding. Some former political prisoners reported psychological abuse and being forced to share a cell with violent criminals. The law permits family and friends to bring detainees food and hygiene products and to send them parcels by mail, but this was frequently not allowed.

As of October 2012 authorities reported that, of the approximately 31,700 persons incarcerated nationwide, approximately 24,900 were adult inmates in penal colonies (prisons), while 633 were adult inmates in the highest-security prisons (with very limited privileges), and 272 were minors in juvenile penal colonies. Approximately 5,800 persons were incarcerated in pretrial detention and other facilities. Approximately 4,500 other persons were held in a form of internal exile (khimiya) in 2011. Persons sentenced to khimiya were allowed to work outside detention facilities but were required to return to prison barracks, where they lived under strict conditions and supervision.

There were isolated reports that police placed underage suspects in pretrial detention facility cells together with adult suspects and former convicts. Juvenile prisoners were held separately from adults at juvenile penal colonies, arrest houses, and pretrial holding facilities. In general conditions for female and juvenile prisoners were slightly better than for male prisoners.

Overcrowding of holding facilities and prisons continued to be a problem, although an amnesty reduced the number of inmates. Ministry of Internal Affairs officials dismissed reports of overcrowding.

On April 22, human rights defender Aleh Volchak filed a complaint with the UN Human Rights Committee about dehumanizing conditions at a short-term holding facility in Minsk. He served several sentences at the facility and cited overcrowding; poor ventilation and lighting; lack of beds, bedding and toiletries; and damp and germ-infected walls.

According to human rights NGOs and former prisoners, authorities routinely abused prisoners and in isolated cases beat or tortured them to death. For example, on August 4, the administration of pretrial holding facility #1 in Minsk informed the family of 21-year-old Ihar Ptichkin that Ptichkin had died in detention of a heart attack. Authorities had previously sentenced Ptichkin to three months in prison for driving with a suspended license. On July 30, he was placed in a holding facility. According to human rights monitoring groups and his family, Ptichkin suffered tooth pain and requested medical assistance, which was denied. When Ptichkin's cellmates protested, a prison riot force reportedly brutally beat Ptichkin, which allegedly led to his death. Ptichkin's family recorded extensive bruises and injuries to his body. After his family filed a number of complaints, the Investigations Committee launched an investigation, including another medical examination of Ptichkin's death. Authorities subsequently charged a prison medical worker with negligence that resulted in Ptichkin's death. The case remained ongoing at year's end.

On at least two occasions during the year, political prisoner Mikalai Autukhovich, an entrepreneur and anticorruption activist from Vaukavysk, cut his stomach to protest prison administration pressure. Autukhovich claimed prison authorities falsely accused him of violating prison regulations, after which they punished him. In January 2012 the Brest Regional Prosecutor's Office refused to open a criminal investigation into reports of his mistreatment. Officials stated that during their inspection it was "not possible" to determine that Autukhovich had suffered systematic dehumanizing treatment or that prison authorities compelled him to attempt suicide in 2011.

Credible sources maintained that prison administrations employed other inmates to intimidate political prisoners and compel confessions. They also reported that authorities neither explained nor protected political prisoners' legal rights and excessively penalized inmates for all minor violation of the prison rules. For example, on February 8, political prisoner and former presidential candidate Mikalai Statkevich reportedly told his wife that in order to pressure him to sign a pardon request for release, the prison administration attempted to place a "specially trained and aggressive former security officer known for abusing and beating cellmates" into his cell.

Corruption in prisons was a serious problem, and observers noted that parole often depended on bribes to prison personnel or a prisoner's political affiliation.

Former prisoners reported limited access to medical care, unqualified medical personnel, and fabricated medical checkups. Observers believed tuberculosis, pneumonia, HIV/AIDS, and other communicable diseases were consequently widespread in prisons. According to domestic human rights groups, tuberculosis infection in prisons exceeded by many times the national average, and the death rate from tuberculosis among inmates was 1.3 times above the national average. The Ministry of Internal Affairs reported that, as of the end of December 2012, 836 prisoners suffered from active tuberculosis. Authorities continued their practice of isolating certain prisoners, particularly inmates with HIV/AIDS and foreign citizens. According to official data, at the end of 2010 there were 1,098 inmates with HIV/AIDS, who accounted for 15 percent of the total reported number of persons with HIV/AIDS in the country.

Administration: Recordkeeping on prisoners was adequate and overseen by the Department of Corrections under the Ministry of Internal Affairs.

Authorities used several alternatives to prison sentences for nonviolent offenders. The most common alternative sentences included partial house arrest, restrictions on freedom of movement, and khimiya (internal exile, see above). In May 2012 an official with the Investigation Committee reported that the number of individuals, especially first-time offenders for nonviolent crimes, who received alternative sentences during the period January through March 2012 was six times higher than for the same period in 2011.

Authorities claimed to have conducted annual or more frequent investigations and monitoring of prison and detention center conditions. Human rights groups, however, asserted that such inspections, even if they did occur, lacked any credibility given the absence of an ombudsman and the inability of human rights advocates to visit prisons or provide consultations to prisoners.

Prisoners and detainees had limited access to visitors, and denial of meetings with families was a common punishment for disciplinary violations. Political prisoners were often denied meetings with families as a means of pressure and intimidation. For example, between his marriage in December 2012 and his release on August 28, 2013, authorities allowed political prisoner Zmitser Dashkevich only one conversation with his spouse: a two-hour discussion on January 9, which occurred through glass and was monitored by prison authorities. In November prison authorities denied Mikalai Autukhovich a scheduled meeting with his mother.

Although the law provides for freedom of religion, and there were no reports of egregious infringements, authorities generally prevented prisoners from holding religious services and performing ceremonies that did not comply with prison regulations. A number of prisons had designated Orthodox facilities, and requests from prisoners of other faiths and denominations to invite clergy were generally accepted.

Former prisoners credibly reported that their complaints to higher authorities were often censored or not forwarded by prison officials, and that prison administrators either ignored or selectively considered requests for investigation of alleged abuses. Complaints could result in retaliation against prisoners who spoke out, including humiliation, death threats, or other forms of punishment.

Independent Monitoring: Authorities did not permit independent monitoring of penal institutions. Despite numerous requests to the Ministries of Internal Affairs and Justice, government officials continued to refuse to meet with human rights advocates or approve requests to visit detention facilities. On April 1, the prominent, yet unregistered, human rights NGO Vyasna released a report on penal system legislation and the treatment of prisoners across the country. In October the prison-monitoring organization Platforma released a report on prison conditions in the country. Human rights advocates based their reports on analyses of legislation, including the protection of freedoms and human rights in prisons, practices of application and enforcement of laws, and information provided by former prisoners, defense lawyers, and families.

BELARUS

d. Arbitrary Arrest or Detention

The law limits arbitrary detention, but the government did not respect these limits. Authorities continued to arrest individuals for political reasons and to use administrative measures to detain political activists before, during, and after protests.

Role of the Police and Security Apparatus

The Ministry of Internal Affairs exercises authority over the police, but the KGB, the Financial Investigations Department of the State Control Committee, the Investigation Committee, and presidential security services also exercise police functions. The president also has the authority to subordinate all security bodies to his personal command. Impunity among law enforcement personnel remained a serious problem. Individuals have the right to report police abuse to a prosecutor, although the government often did not investigate reported abuses or hold perpetrators accountable.

Arrest Procedures and Treatment of Detainees

By law police must request permission from a prosecutor to detain a person for more than three hours, but police usually ignored this procedure and routinely detained and arrested individuals without warrants. Authorities may hold a criminal suspect for up to 10 days without filing formal charges and for up to 18 months after filing charges. Under the law prosecutors, investigators, and security service agencies have the authority to extend detention without consulting a judge. Detainees have the right to petition the court system regarding the legality of their detention, but authorities frequently suppressed or ignored such appeals.

Arbitrary Arrest: During the year authorities routinely detained or arrested dozens of individuals, including opposition figures, members of the independent media, social media activists, and civil society activists, for reasons widely considered to be politically motivated. Authorities used administrative measures to detain political activists before, during, and after planned demonstrations and protests.

On April 26, following a government-sanctioned Chernobyl commemoration march, authorities detained several opposition activists and sentenced them to jail terms. Alyaksandr Tarnahurski and Dzmitry Charnyak, activists from the unregistered opposition group European Belarus, were sentenced to 10 days in jail for participating in the march.

Country Reports on Human Rights Practices for 2013
United States Department of State • Bureau of Democracy, Human Rights and Labor

On June 25, authorities sentenced Anatol Shumchanka, a small business activist and leader of the registered "Perspektyva" business association, to five days in jail for organizing an "unsanctioned gathering." He was arrested after meeting with market vendors staging a strike in Minsk against new sales regulations.

On September 14, police arrested at least 18 activists, friends, and family members of 21-year-old Ihar Ptichkin, who died in prison of reported beatings, as well as three independent journalists on their way to commemorate his death at the jail entrance. Authorities detained the journalists, searched them for three hours, and released them without charge. Authorities fined five persons up to 600,000 Belarusian rubles ($64) on September 16 and 18 and gave an official warning to Ptichkin's pregnant sister. On November 14 and 15, a court sentenced Alyaksandr Danilau and Andrei Bandarenka to five days in jail for taking part in the unsanctioned gathering.

Pretrial Detention: Authorities may hold a criminal suspect for up to 10 days without filing formal charges. Prior to being charged, the law provides detainees with no access to their families or to outside food and medical supplies, both of which are vital given poor conditions. Police routinely held persons for the full 10-day period before charging them.

Police often detained individuals for several hours, ostensibly to confirm their identity; fingerprinted them; and then released them without charges. Police and security forces frequently used this tactic to detain members of the democratic opposition and demonstrators, to prevent the distribution of leaflets and newspapers, or as a pretext to break up civil society meetings and events.

On May 9, authorities detained Pavel Vinahradaw, leader of the youth wing of the "Tell the Truth!" movement, to prevent him from meeting opposition activist Uladzimir Yaromenak upon his release from detention. He was held for nine hours without charge. On May 31, Vinahradaw was similarly detained without charge for 12 hours to prevent him from staging a protest in Minsk at a high-level meeting of the Commonwealth of Independent States.

On March 22, authorities in Vitsyebsk arrested two members of the Belarusian Popular Front, Kanstantsin Smolikau and Leanid Autukhou, to prevent their commemorating the 95th anniversary of the short-lived Belarusian National Republic on March 25. They were subsequently sentenced to five days in jail.

Authorities arrested several other opposition activists before and after events celebrating the anniversary.

Amnesty: An amnesty, which aimed to reduce the prison population, began in July 2012 and was completed on January 11. Under the amnesty, the government released 3,059 convicts from prison, released another 1,167 from serving "khimiya," and reduced by one year the sentences of 6,064. No political prisoners were released under the amnesty.

e. Denial of Fair Public Trial

The constitution provides for an independent judiciary, but authorities did not respect judicial independence. Corruption, inefficiency, and political interference with judicial decisions were widespread. Courts convicted individuals on false and politically motivated charges brought by prosecutors, and observers believed that senior government leaders and local authorities dictated the outcomes of trials.

According to the human rights monitoring organization Platforma, prosecutors wielded excessive and imbalanced authority because they may extend detention without the permission of judges. They also noted a power imbalance between the prosecution and the defense. Defense lawyers were unable to examine investigation files, be present during investigations and interrogations, or examine evidence against defendants until a prosecutor formally brought the case to court. Lawyers found it difficult to challenge some evidence because technical expertise was under the control of the Prosecutor's Office. According to many defense attorneys, this power imbalance persisted throughout the year, especially in politically motivated criminal and administrative cases. Criminal defendants were exonerated in very few cases during the year.

Under a law amended in April 2012, bar associations are independent, and licensed lawyers can establish private practices or bureaus, but they remained subordinate to the Ministry of Justice. All lawyers must be licensed by the ministry and renew their licenses every five years. Although previously the law prohibited attorneys from engaging in private practice, private legal companies were allowed to provide legal assistance and advice to private companies and represent their clients in economic courts.

In March 2012 the Minsk city bar association expelled Andrei Varvashevich, a lawyer for former presidential candidate Andrei Sannikau. Varvashevich has not been permitted to renew his license. During the year there were no new disbarments, but no debarred lawyers had their license restored. The Justice Ministry previously accused lawyers defending politically motivated detainees of distorting information about the investigations of their clients, their state of health, and their conditions of detention. In 2012 the ministry announced that all licensed lawyers, excluding junior staff, had to pass extraordinary performance reviews to renew their licenses. The law authorizes the ministry to advise lawyers and bar members on whom to elect as chairpersons.

Trial Procedures

The law provides for the presumption of innocence. Nevertheless, the lack of judicial independence, the practice of state media to report on high-profile cases as if guilt were already certain, and widespread practices of limiting the right of self-defense frequently placed the burden of proving one's innocence on the defendant.

The law also provides for public trials, but trials occasionally were closed and frequently were held in judges' offices, where attendance was severely limited. Judges adjudicate all trials; there is no system of trial by jury. For the most serious cases, two civilian advisers assist the judge.

The law provides defendants the right to attend proceedings, confront witnesses, and present evidence on their own behalf, but authorities did not always respect these rights.

The law provides for access to legal counsel for detainees and requires that courts appoint a lawyer for those who cannot afford one. Most judges and prosecutors were not fluent in Belarusian and rejected motions for interpreters. The law provides for the right to choose legal representation freely; however, a presidential decree prohibits NGO members who are lawyers from representing individuals other than members of their organizations in court. The government's disbarment of attorneys who represented political opponents of the regime limited defendants' choice of counsel in high-profile political cases. The government's actions further forced lawyers to limit their contacts with media and refrain from public comments regarding their clients' cases.

Those charged in connection with the December 2010 demonstrations had very limited access to lawyers, and authorities did not allow any of these detainees to meet in private with their lawyers at holding facilities. Some lawyers openly stated in 2011 that authorities obstructed them from seeing clients in connection with the 2010 demonstrations.

Courts often allowed statements obtained by use of force and threats of bodily harm during interrogations to be used against defendants.

Defendants have the right to appeal court decisions, and most defendants did so. Nevertheless, appeals courts upheld the verdicts of the lower courts in the vast majority of cases, including in all criminal cases connected with post-election demonstrations.

Political Prisoners and Detainees

Local and international human rights organizations reported several different lists of political prisoners in the country. These included individuals serving prison time or partial house arrest at the year's end. The independent human rights monitoring NGO "Vyasna" reported that there were 11 political prisoners in the country. Government officials referenced "so-called political prisoners" but denied that they received harsher treatment in detention facilities. Many of those pardoned reported pressure to sign pardon requests, and most were subsequently still unable to exercise some civil and political rights.

Several prominent prisoners' prison terms expired during the year, including Dzmitry Dashkevich, Aliaksandr Frantskevich, Vasil Parfyankow, and Paval Sevyarynets. Former presidential candidate Uladzimir Nyaklyaeu, his aides Alyaksandr Fyaduta and Syarhei Vaznyak, and independent journalist and the spouse of former presidential candidate Andrei Sannikau, Iryna Khalip, served out their two-year suspended and conditional sentences. Following their release, most were unable to exercise their full civil and political rights. They continued to face restrictions on their freedom of movement and were subject to police supervision. For example, in December police reportedly warned Dashkevich that the conditions of his parole could be tightened if he did not "improve" his behavior, a reference to his continuing political activities. Dashkevich was subject to an enforced curfew and could not move from his place of residence, among other restrictions.

Prominent prisoners, including former presidential candidate Mikalai Statkevich and Malady Front leader Eduard Lobau, reportedly faced mistreatment and severe pressure in jail.

Ales Byalyatski, chairman of Vyasna, remained imprisoned on politically motivated tax evasion charges related to his human rights activities.

Ales Mikhalevich, a former presidential candidate charged in a criminal case related to the 2010 postelection demonstration, remained abroad, where he fled in 2011. During the year authorities notified Mikhalevich that he could be informed of the status of his case only in person.

Two other individuals whom prosecutors called "anarchists" remained in prison at year's end. During their court hearings, the defendants reported threats against associates and family members to compel them to testify against them, as well as pressure to sign confessions. Leading local human rights groups, including Vyasna and the Belarusian Helsinki Committee (BHC), either recognized these individuals as prisoners of conscience or noted serious due process violations that required at the very least a retrial.

Authorities also maintained control over some of those prisoners who already had been released. For example, on August 20 authorities sentenced Uladzimir Yaromenak, an activist of the Young Front opposition movement and former political prisoner, to three months in jail on charges of violating preventive supervision restrictions. On November 12, the Minsk City Court denied Yaromenak's appeal and upheld the three-month jail sentence. On December 11, Yaromenak began serving his three-month sentence.

Civil Judicial Procedures and Remedies

The law provides that individuals can file lawsuits seeking damages for a human rights violation, but the civil judiciary was not independent and was rarely impartial in such matters.

f. Arbitrary Interference with Privacy, Family, Home, or Correspondence

The law prohibits such actions, but the government did not respect these prohibitions. Authorities used wiretapping, video surveillance, and a network of informers that deprived persons of privacy.

By law persons who obstruct law enforcement personnel in the performance of their duties can be penalized or charged with an administrative offense, even if the "duties" are inconsistent with the law. "Obstruction" could include any effort to prevent KGB or law enforcement officers from entering the premises of a company, establishment, or organization; refusing to allow KGB audits; or denying or restricting KGB access to information systems and databases.

The law requires a warrant before, or immediately after, conducting a search, but the KGB and riot police entered homes, conducted searches, and read mail without warrants. The KGB has the authority to enter any building at any time, as long as it applies for a warrant within 24 hours after the entry.

Security forces continued to target prominent opposition and civil society leaders with arbitrary searches and interrogations at border crossings and airports. For example, on September 14, authorities detained and searched without explanation Natalya Mankouskaya, GayBelarus LGBT rights group coordinator and human rights advocate, at a border upon her return from Ukraine. She was released without charge.

While the law prohibits authorities from intercepting telephone and other communications without a prosecutor's order, authorities routinely monitored residences, telephones, and computers. Nearly all opposition political figures and many prominent members of civil society groups reported that authorities monitored their conversations and activities.

The law allows the KGB, Ministry of Internal Affairs, special security services, financial intelligence personnel, and certain border guard detachments to use wiretaps. Wiretaps require the permission of a prosecutor, but the lack of prosecutorial independence rendered this requirement meaningless.

The Ministry of Communications has the authority to terminate the telephone service of persons who violate their telephone contracts, and such contracts prohibit the use of telephone services for purposes contrary to state interests and public order. Cellular telephone providers are banned from selling cellular telephone cards to customers who do not produce their passports or to foreigners who are not registered with local migration services.

Authorities continued to harass family members of NGO leaders and civil society and opposition activists through selective application of the law.

Section 2. Respect for Civil Liberties, Including:

a. Freedom of Speech and Press

The constitution provides for freedom of speech and press. Nevertheless, the government did not respect these rights and enforced numerous laws to control and censor the public and the media. Moreover, the state press propagated views in support of Lukashenka and official policies.

Freedom of Speech: Individuals could not criticize the government publicly or discuss matters of general public interest without fear of possible reprisal. Authorities videotaped political meetings, conducted frequent identity checks, and used other forms of intimidation. Wearing masks, displaying unregistered or opposition flags and symbols, and displaying placards bearing messages deemed threatening to the government or public order also were prohibited.

For example, authorities sentenced Ruslan Mirzoev to seven days of administrative arrest for posting videos online that detailed the daily life of workers at the Minsk Automobile Plant. He was fired from his job in July.

On August 16, a psychiatric commission at a hospital in Vityebsk concluded that Doctor Ihar Pastnow should receive forced psychiatric treatment after he frequently criticized local government authorities for underfunding in the state medical system and posted critical videos on the internet. Pastnow accused Alyaksandr Kosinets, head of the regional government, of wasting public funds. In September Pastnow was released from involuntary treatment.

On September 30, authorities fined four joggers taking part in a charity run in Minsk approximately 1.3 million rubles ($140) each for reportedly wearing T-shirts with the image of imprisoned 2010 presidential candidate Mikolai Statkeivich. Yawhen Naporka, Maksim Dubowski, Andrey Vislovich, and Kiryl Zhyvalovich were charged with "standing in front of the stage and people, wearing T-shirts with images."

On November 3, authorities arrested Yury Rubtsow, a member of the Independent Union of Electronic Industry Workers (REP), during a government-sanctioned commemoration event at the Kurapaty Forest massacre site for the Dzyady holiday and sentenced him to three days in jail for wearing a T-shirt bearing anti-Lukashenka slogans. Upon his release, authorities re-arrested him for wearing the same T-shirt and he was re-released only after removing the shirt.

The law also limits free speech by criminalizing actions such as giving information to a foreigner about the political, economic, social, military, or international situation of the country that authorities deem false or derogatory.

Press Freedoms: Government restriction of press freedom severely limited access to information and often resulted in self-censorship by the media. Appearances by opposition politicians on state media were limited to those required by law during election campaigns. In 2012 they were further limited by official censorship during the parliamentary election. Authorities warned, fined, detained, interrogated, or jailed members of the media and harassed bloggers who publicly criticized the government. Under the law the government may close a publication after two warnings in one year for violating a range of restrictions on the press. In addition regulations give authorities arbitrary power to prohibit or censor reporting. The Information Ministry can suspend periodicals or newspapers for three months without a court ruling. The law also prohibits the media from disseminating information on behalf of unregistered political parties, trade unions, and NGOs.

During the 2012 parliamentary election campaign, state-controlled media outlets censored speeches by democratic opposition candidates, a step back from the 2010 presidential elections, when candidates were allowed to appear live.

The Information Ministry continued to deny registration to many independent media outlets. In spite of the lack of registration, independent media, including newspapers, magazines, and internet news websites, sought to provide objective and independent coverage of events. They operated, however, under repressive media laws, and most faced discriminatory publishing and distribution policies, including limiting access to government officials and press briefings, controlling the size of press runs of papers, and raising the cost of printing. During the year the government confiscated numerous independent and opposition newspapers and seized leaflets and other materials deemed to have been printed illegally. Authorities also often fined distributors of independent press publications.

State-owned media, which were extremely biased and served as a propaganda arm of the regime, dominated the information field and maintained the highest circulation through generous subsidies and preferences. There is no countrywide private television. The state-owned postal system, Belposhta, and the state-owned kiosk system, Belsayuzdruk, continued to refuse to deliver or sell numerous independent newspapers that covered politics.

Although authorities continued to allow the circulation of *Narodnaya Volya* and *Nasha Niva*, two independent national newspapers, through state distribution systems, they remained subject to restrictions and financial penalties.

Several independent newspapers, including *Vitsyebski Kuryer*, printed materials in Russia because domestic printing presses (almost all of which were state-owned) refused to print them. Other independent newspapers, such as *Salidarnasc*, *BDG*, and *Bobruysky Kuryer*, disseminated internet-only versions due to printing and distribution restrictions.

International media continued to operate in the country, but not without interference and prior censorship. Euronews and the Russian channels First Channel, NTV, and RTR were generally available, although only through paid cable services in many parts of the country and then with a lag time that allowed the removal of news deemed undesirable by authorities. At times authorities blocked, censored, or replaced their international news programs with local programming. Satellite broadcasts from other countries, including Poland and Lithuania, could be received in parts of the country, usually along the border.

Violence and Harassment: Authorities continued to routinely harass, arrest, and assault journalists.

During the year suspended sentences against several members of the Belarusian Association of Journalists (BAJ) expired. These sentences were the result of the 2011 convictions of several BAJ journalists on charges of "participating in mass disturbances" or organizing activities that "violated public order" as a result of their work on presidential campaigns in 2010. Security forces continued to monitor the activities of a number of journalists following the expiration of their suspended sentences.

Authorities raided offices of media organizations. For example, on April 29, Radio Racyja journalist Ryhor Sapyazhynski reported that unknown individuals entered the Radio Racyja offices over the weekend and allegedly accessed studio records and journalists' computers.

Security forces continually hampered efforts of independent journalists to cover demonstrations and protests in Minsk and across the country. For example, on April 26, following a government-sanctioned Chernobyl commemoration march, authorities detained two independent journalists who covered the march and sentenced them to jail terms. Authorities sentenced Henadz Barbarych and Alyaksandr Yarashevich, reporters for Polish-based Radio Racyja, to three days in jail for failing to comply with police orders. Authorities also allegedly searched their office computers.

Harassment of Belarusian and foreign journalists was also common.

On January 23, the Foreign Ministry refused to renew official accreditation to Pavel Svyardlow, a European Radio for Belarus correspondent. On August 1, the ministry granted Svyardlow a new accreditation.

Censorship or Content Restrictions: The government obliged the vast majority of publications to exercise self-censorship. The government tightly controlled the content of state broadcast and print media. Local independent television stations operated in some areas and reported local news, although most were under government pressure to forego reporting on national and sensitive issues or risk censorship.

Only state-run radio and the state-run television networks were allowed to broadcast nationwide. The government continued to use its monopoly of television and radio broadcasting to disseminate its version of events and minimize all opposing viewpoints. State television broadcast crudely propagandistic documentaries targeting opposition and often civil society actors that contained surveillance footage and wiretap transcripts that appeared to be supplied by the security services. Authorities banned state media from citing works and broadcasting music by independent local and well-known foreign musicians, artists, writers, and painters who were named on an alleged, unofficial nationwide "blacklist" for speaking in support of political prisoners and opposition or democratic activists.

Local authorities frequently warned independent editors and journalists to avoid reporting on certain topics and not to criticize the government. Authorities harassed bloggers for the same reasons. Authorities also warned businesses not to advertise in newspapers that criticized the government. As a result, independent media outlets operated under severe budgetary constraints.

Journalists reporting for international media that gave extensive coverage to the country, such as the Warsaw-based independent satellite channel Belsat TV and Radio Racyja, were unable to receive press accreditation and thus continued to receive warnings from the Prosecutor's Office for working without it.

On March 26, the Foreign Ministry again denied accreditation to Belsat TV and accused Belsat journalists of repeatedly violating Belarusian laws in their work.

<u>Libel Laws/National Security</u>: Libel is a criminal offense. There are large fines and prison sentences of up to four years for defaming or insulting the president. Penalties for defamation of character make no distinction between private and public persons. A public figure who is criticized for poor performance while in office may sue both the journalist and the media outlet that disseminated the critical report.

For example, on July 26, authorities sentenced playwright Andrei Karelin to a 10-million Belarusian ruble ($1,066) fine for two comments he made on an internet portal that were critical of police officers. Karelin was convicted for "insulting an officer on duty" after claiming police officers did not offer him proper assistance when unnamed assailants attacked and beat him in Minsk in May.

On August 17, police in Homel region raided the apartment of Henadz Zhuleha, a blogger and civil society activist, after he filmed the house of the head of the Svetlahorsk District Executive Committee and posted the video online. Police confiscated his computer for further examination.

On September 23, a Hrodna court lifted all restrictions, including a criminal record, against independent journalist and former political prisoner Andrzej Poczobut. The ruling came upon the expiration of his two-year probationary sentence. In 2011 a Hrodna court sentenced Poczobut to a three-year suspended sentence for slandering the president. In 2012 authorities arrested him on new charges but subsequently released him. During this time period authorities prohibited Poczobut from leaving the country.

Authorities also frequently cited national security as grounds for censorship of media.

Internet Freedom

The government continued to interfere with internet freedom by actively monitoring e-mail and internet chat rooms. While individuals and groups were generally able to engage in the peaceful expression of views via the internet, including by e-mail, all who did so risked possible legal and personal repercussions. Opposition activists faced the likelihood that their e-mails and other web-based communications would be monitored. Moreover, government providers blocked independent and opposition websites during major political events, such as demonstrations and previous national elections.

The independent online research agency Gemius Belarus reported that as of November 2012 the number of internet users reached approximately 4,460,000 persons, or 13 percent more than in 2011. More than 80 percent of those using the internet did so daily, and the level of internet penetration was approximately 55 percent.

The authorities monitored internet traffic. By law the telecommunications monopoly, Beltelekam, and other organizations authorized by the government have the exclusive right to maintain internet domains.

A 2010 edict issued by Lukashenka requires registration of service providers and internet websites, establishes restrictions on access to sites containing "extremist activity" (which many activists believed could be interpreted to include government opponents), and requires the collection of information on users at internet cafes. It requires service providers to store data on the internet use of individuals for a year and provide that information to law enforcement agencies upon their request. Violations of the edict are punishable by jail time.

The edict restricts access to websites whose content includes "extremist activities;" materials related to illicit weapons, explosives, and drugs; trafficking in persons; pornography; and the promotion of violence. It requires service providers to eliminate access to these subjects from government offices, educational facilities, and cultural institutions if ordered to do so by the KGB, prosecutor general, the Presidential Administration's Operation and Analytical Center, or other state agencies. The edict does not block access from private sites such as homes or private companies. According to credible sources, the list, which was not released publicly, contained approximately 80 websites, including opposition portals Charter 97 and Belarusian Partisan. Internet service providers are required to update the list on a daily basis. Decisions to restrict access to internet sources may be appealed to the courts.

State companies and organizations, which included the workplaces of 80 percent of the country's workers, reportedly had internet filters. In response to the government's interference and internet restrictions, many opposition groups and independent newspapers switched to internet domains operating outside the country. The few remaining independent media sites with domestic ".BY" (Belarus) domain suffixes practiced self-censorship.

In December the prosecutor general responded to an inquiry by the human rights organization Vyasna and stated that the government blocks the Vyasna website on computers at government buildings and other official institutions because the group is not registered, rendering its activities illegal.

On several occasions cyber attacks of unknown origin temporarily disabled independent news portals and social networking sites. For example, on April 25, a cyber attack targeted Vyasna's website, resulting in changes to their website content. Distributed denial-of-service cyber attacks also targeted the Belarusian Association of Journalists' website the following day.

The government continued to collect and obtain personally identifiable information on independent journalists and democratic activists during raids and by confiscating computer equipment.

Academic Freedom and Cultural Events

The government restricted academic freedom and cultural events. Educational institutions were required to teach an official state ideology that combined reverence for the achievements of the former Soviet Union and Belarus under the leadership of Lukashenka. Use of the word "academic" was restricted, and NGOs were prohibited from including the word "academy" in their titles. Opportunities to receive a higher education in the Belarusian language in the majority of fields of study were scarce. The administrations of higher educational institutions made no effort to accommodate students wishing to study in Belarusian-language classes.

Authorities harassed, intimidated, and dismissed teachers and professors on political grounds. For example, in June university administrations dismissed Valyantsina Alinevich, a professor at Belarusian State Economic University in Minsk and mother of political prisoner Ihar Alinevich, and Valery Beraziyenka, a professor at Belarusian-Russian University in Mahilyow and member of an opposition party.

Government-mandated textbooks contained a heavily propagandized version of history and other subjects. All schools, including private institutions, were obligated to follow state directives to inculcate the official ideology and could not be led by opposition members. The education minister has the right to appoint and dismiss the heads of private educational institutions.

The Belarusian Republican Youth Union (BRYU), an official organization modeled on the Soviet-era Komsomol, urged university students to join the BRYU to receive benefits and dormitory rooms. Local authorities also pressured BRYU members to campaign on behalf of government candidates. In addition authorities at times reportedly pressured students to act as informants for the country's security services. High school students feared that they would not be allowed to enroll in universities without BRYU membership, and university students reported that proof of BRYU membership often was required to register for popular courses or to receive a dormitory room. Universities also offered BRYU members discounts on tuition.

According to an Education Ministry directive, educational institutions may expel students who engage in antigovernment or unsanctioned political activity and must ensure the proper ideological education of students. School officials, however, cited poor academic performance or absence from classes as the official reason for expulsions.

The government continued to ban teachers and democratic activists from promoting the wider use of the Belarusian language and the preservation of Belarusian culture. For example, a number of universities across the country continued not to enroll students in their undergraduate Belarusian linguistic programs for teachers of the Belarusian language and literature, citing low demand and a low number of applications in recent years.

The government also restricted cultural events. It continued to force opposition theater and music groups out of public venues and into bars and private apartments by banning their performances. Authorities also suppressed unofficial commemorations of historical events. In January Lukashenka stated that he was not aware of any blacklist for musicians or artists. He suggested that musicians are punished for "spitting on the country" and accused them of accepting payments from outside groups.

On April 19, the administration of the Youth Popular Music Theater cancelled an April 24 concert in commemoration of prominent national revival activist Aryna Vyachorka, the wife of opposition politician Vintsuk Vyachorka.

On August 8, Uladzimir Shcherban, a director of the Belarus Free Theater (BFT), wrote that police visited a BFT performance and recorded the passport information of attendees. Such incidents occurred at least four times during the year, including on September 14, when police disrupted another BFT play, recorded the passport information of attendees, and ordered everyone to disperse.

The government also restricted the activities of a nonofficial writers union and extensively supported the progovernment Union of Writers of Belarus. Authorities harassed distributors of books authored by critical and independent writers or written in the Belarusian language.

On February 6, plainclothes policemen disrupted a book launch event featuring a novel by poet and 2010 presidential candidate Uladzimir Nyaklyaeu in Minsk. A policeman warned Andrei Khadanovich, chairman of the Belarusian PEN Center and the Union of Belarusian Writers, that the event was unscheduled and asked him to end his presentation of Nyaklyaeu's work. Nyaklyaeu remained at the venue and signed autographs under the watch of plainclothes policemen.

On April 18, a judge of the Ashmyany District Court declared a book featuring photos selected for the 2011 Belarus Press Photo contest to be "extremist material." The judge ordered Vadzim Zamirouski, Yuliya Darashkevich, and Alyaksandr Vasyukevich, the contest's co-organizers, to pay 217,500 rubles ($23) each in litigation costs. On September 23, the Information Ministry stripped the Minsk-based private Lohvinau Publishing House of its license for its role in publishing the photobook. The Supreme Economic Court of Belarus subsequently rejected a lawsuit brought by Lohvinau Publishing House to restore their license. In November 2012 authorities seized 41 copies of the book from the contest co-organizers when they returned from a trip to Lithuania. The court ordered the destruction of these 41 confiscated copies.

On May 22, the Information Ministry re-registered the Belarusian language literary magazine *Arche*. In September 2012 authorities arrested editor chief Valer Bulhakau and confiscated more than 5,000 books written in the Belarusian language. Bulhakau fled the country, and authorities subsequently froze *Arche* magazine's bank accounts.

On September 3, a commission of experts ruled that political prisoner Ales Byalyatski's book about Belarusian literature, which he wrote in detention, "caus[ed] harm to the image of Belarus." Customs officers in Ashmyany confiscated 40 copies of the book from Byalyatski's associate Tatsyana Ravyaka on July 3 and forwarded them to the commission for examination.

b. Freedom of Peaceful Assembly and Association

Freedom of Assembly

The constitution provides for freedom of peaceful assembly; however, the government severely restricted this right. Only registered political parties, trade unions, and NGOs could request permission to hold a demonstration of more than 1,000 persons. Authorities usually denied requests by independent and opposition groups. A general atmosphere of repression and the threat of imprisonment exercised a chilling effect on potential protest organizers. This resulted in fewer demonstrations and contributed to fewer forceful dispersals of peaceful protestors than in previous years.

The law criminalizes participation in the activities of unregistered NGOs, training persons to demonstrate, financing public demonstrations, or soliciting foreign assistance "to the detriment" of the country. In 2011 the law was amended to also prohibit announcing demonstrations, including via the internet or social networks, before they are approved by authorities. Violations are punishable by up to three years in prison.

For example, on June 1, the Shchychyn District Police Department began criminal proceedings against Aliaksei Shchadrou, a Catholic lay worker, for running an unregistered shelter for homeless people. He was charged with organizing "at his place of residence an unregistered religious organization and secured the condition for its functioning without registration in accordance with the procedure established in law." On July 15, Shchadrou appealed against the charge to the prosecutor of Shchychyn District, arguing that the case against him was unconstitutional. All charges were dropped in September after local authorities registered Shchadrou's charitable organization.

Authorities employed a variety of means to discourage demonstrations, disperse them, minimize their impact, and punish the participants. Organizers must apply at least 15 days in advance for permission to conduct a public demonstration, rally, or meeting, and government officials are required to respond no later than five days prior to the scheduled event. Authorities, however, generally refused permits to opposition groups or granted permits only for demonstrations held far from city centers. Authorities used intimidation and threats to discourage persons from participating in demonstrations, openly videotaped participants, and imposed heavy fines or jail sentences on participants in unsanctioned demonstrations.

In May authorities rejected nearly 60 applications for permission for opposition United Civic Party activists to stage small demonstrations on May 7 to mark the anniversary of the 1999-2000 disappearances of former interior minister Yury

Zakharanka, former central election commission head Viktar Hanchar, businessman Anatol Krasowski, and journalist Dzmitry Zavadski.

In August and September, local authorities denied permission for activists from the opposition Belarusian Popular Front to stage demonstrations on September 8 against the establishment of a Russian military base in the country. Authorities denied at least 17 separate applications.

On many occasions police and other security officials beat and detained demonstrators before, during, and after unsanctioned peaceful demonstrations. Numerous protest participants were detained, fined, and sentenced to periods of up to 15 days in administrative detention. Authorities fined opposition activists and members of NGOs for participating in unauthorized protests.

For example, on April 26, police beat and arrested Ihar Trukhanovich, a member of an alleged anarchist group, for taking part in an officially sanctioned event commemorating the anniversary of the 1986 Chernobyl nuclear accident.

On September 27, authorities sentenced youth activist Paval Vinahradau to 15 days in prison for violating regulations on holding demonstrations after he displayed swine heads in downtown Minsk adorned with signs critical of Lukashenka and authorities.

Police even suppressed small authorized demonstrations.

Police also used preemptive arrest and detention to prevent democratic activists' participation in protests. For example, authorities took various measures to deter prodemocracy activists from celebrating the March 25 anniversary of the country's 1918 declaration of independence (an event the government does not recognize), although Minsk city authorities authorized the demonstration. Authorities blocked a number of opposition activists in their residences early in the morning, warned many regional opposition activists against traveling to Minsk to participate in the demonstration, or detained them while they were en route to demonstration sites, to prevent them from leading demonstrations. For example, on March 24 police in Polatsk prevented Uladzimir Kapelkin, a member of the opposition Belarusian Christian Democracy party, from traveling to Minsk to attend the celebrations. Plainclothes policemen briefly detained at least six demonstrators following the event.

On April 19, authorities detained four environmentalists and a prominent antinuclear activist ahead of a government-sanctioned Chernobyl anniversary demonstration in Minsk. Iryna Sukhi, Volha Kanavalava, Vasil Semyanikhin, and Kanstantsin Kirylenka were arrested and held at a district police station for three hours, which prevented them from joining the demonstration. Authorities arrested Mikalay Ulasevich on the way to the same demonstration. The previous day district police officers warned Ulasevich against any illegal activities in connection with his participation in the event.

Authorities rejected all requests to conduct events commemorating the third anniversary of the 2010 crackdown on postelection demonstrations and the continued detention of political prisoners.

Freedom of Association

The law provides for freedom of association, but the government restricted it and selectively enforced laws and registration regulations to restrict the operation of independent associations that might criticize the government.

All NGOs, political parties, and trade unions must receive prior approval from the Ministry of Justice to register. A government commission reviews and approves all registration applications; its decisions were based largely on political and ideological compatibility with the government's authoritarian philosophy. Actual registration procedures required applicants to provide the number and names of founders, along with a physical address in a nonresidential building for an office, an extraordinary burden in view of the tight financial straits of most NGOs and individual property owners' fears of renting space to nonstate groups. Individuals listed as members were vulnerable to retribution. The government's refusal to rent office space to unregistered organizations and the expense of renting private space reportedly forced most organizations to use residential addresses, which could serve as a reason for deregistration.

Following the 2010 crackdown, authorities sought to close any "legal loopholes" they considered beneficial to NGOs. For example, the law on public associations prohibits NGOs from keeping funds at foreign financial institutions for local activities. The law also prohibits NGOs from facilitating provision of any support or benefits from foreign states to civil servants based on their political or religious views or ethnicity, a provision widely believed to be aimed at the Polish minority.

Only registered NGOs can legally accept foreign grants and technical aid. NGOs must receive approval from the Department for Humanitarian Affairs of the Presidential Administration before they can accept such funds as well as register the grants.

The government continued to deny registration to NGOs and political parties on a variety of pretexts, including "technical" problems with applications. Authorities frequently harassed and intimidated individuals who identified themselves as founding members of organizations in an effort to induce them to abandon their membership and thus deprive groups of the number of petitioners necessary for registration. Many of the rejected groups previously had sought and been denied registration on multiple occasions. The government continued deregistering groups during the year.

For example, on June 24 the Justice Ministry denied registration to the NGO "Campaign for Fair Elections." This was the NGO's second registration attempt.

On August 7, the Supreme Court rejected an appeal by the opposition "Tell the Truth!" movement against the Justice Ministry's decision to deny it official registration. This was the movement's third unsuccessful registration attempt.

Authorities continued to issue written warnings to NGOs, political parties, and trade unions, as well as their members. For example, in July the Justice Ministry issued a formal warning to the small business association "Perspektyva" for allegedly violating the Mass Events Law.

Harassment in the form of inspections by security officials and confiscation of political literature continued.

For example, on August 24, police raided the Minsk offices of the opposition "Tell the Truth!" movement and briefly detained about 30 activists participating in a training seminar. Police took the activists' fingerprints, photographed and filmed the offices, and copied the contents of the movement's laptops and cameras. They also seized political flyers and copies of a Lukashenka biography by Valery Karbalevich, a leading independent analyst.

c. Freedom of Religion

See the Department of State's *International Religious Freedom Report* at www.state.gov/j/drl/irf/rpt/.

d. Freedom of Movement, Internally Displaced Persons, Protection of Refugees, and Stateless Persons

The law provides for freedom of movement, including the right to emigrate, but the government at times restricted the right of its citizens to foreign travel. The government cooperated with the Office of the UN High Commissioner for Refugees (UNHCR) and other humanitarian organizations in providing protection and assistance to internally displaced persons, refugees, returning refugees, asylum seekers, stateless persons, and persons of concern.

In-country Movement: Passports serve as a form of national identity document and are required for permanent housing, work, and hotel registration. Police continued to harass individuals who lived at a location other than their legal place of residence indicated in mandatory stamps in their passports.

The law also requires persons who travel to areas within 15 miles of the border to obtain an entrance pass.

Foreign Travel: The government maintained a database of persons who were banned from traveling abroad and, at times, used it to prevent travel of opposition politicians and civil society activists. According to the Ministry of Internal Affairs, the list contained the names of at least 130,000 persons who were prohibited from foreign travel, including those who possessed state secrets, faced criminal prosecution or civil suits, or had outstanding financial commitments. Some persons were informed by letter that their names were in the database; others were informed at border crossings. In certain cases opposition activists either were turned away at the border or detained for lengthy searches.

For example, in January, following police raids on LGBT clubs across the country, authorities seized the passport of Syarhey Androsenka, the leader of LGBT rights group Lambda. Authorities returned his passport three weeks later. On March 27, customs officers detained and searched Androsenka as he returned to the country from Lithuania. Authorities seized his passport yet again and returned it approximately 40 days later; during this interval he was unable to leave the country.

In July 2012 Lukashenka issued orders to ban persons under the KGB's special "preventive" surveillance from traveling abroad. Based on results of preliminary criminal investigations or searches, the KGB is authorized to monitor persons whose activities "may threaten the national security of Belarus, inflict damages to state or public interests, rights, freedoms, and legitimate interests of individuals" and "may result in committing subsequent crimes." The Internal Affairs Ministry and security agencies, border and customs services, and financial investigation departments have a right to place persons on "preventive" surveillance lists. For example, in July 2012 the KGB notified Andrei Bandarenka, the head of the NGO Platforma, that his name was added to the "preventive" register; his name was later removed from the register.

A presidential decree that requires any student who wishes to study abroad to obtain permission from the minister of education was amended in July 2012. Heads of educational institutions are required to issue such permission to their students. The decree, ostensibly intended to counter trafficking in persons, still requires the Ministry of Internal Affairs to track citizens working abroad and obliges employment agencies to report individuals who do not return from abroad as scheduled.

Exile: The law does not allow forced exile, but sources asserted that security forces continued to threaten some opposition members with bodily harm or prosecution if they did not leave the country, and many were in self-imposed exile. For example, authorities allegedly urged independent journalist Iryna Khalip to leave the country after charges against her were dropped in July. Khimiya, a form of internal exile, is permitted for persons convicted of crimes, and authorities employed it during the year.

Many university students who had been expelled or were under threat of expulsion for their political activities opted for self-imposed exile.

Protection of Refugees

Access to Asylum: The law provides for the granting of asylum or refugee status, and the government has established a system for providing protection to refugees.

While all foreigners have the right to apply for asylum, authorities did not grant Russian nationals either refugee status or complementary protection in the country. Under the terms of the Union Treaty with Russia, Russians can legally settle and obtain residence permits in the country based on their Russian citizenship and therefore do not need asylum. Nevertheless, immigration authorities accepted three asylum applications from Russian citizens in 2012, one of which was withdrawn by the applicant.

Refoulement: In addition to refugee status, the country's asylum law provides for complementary protection and protection against refoulement (in the form of temporary residence for a one-year term). In 2012 at least one person applied for extension of complementary protection, which was granted, and five persons were able to extend protection against refoulement for one year.

Refugee Abuse: Asylum seekers have freedom of movement within the country but must reside in the region where they filed their applications for refugee status and in a place known to authorities while their applications are being considered, including during an appeals procedure. Authorities reportedly often encouraged asylum seekers to settle in rural areas. Change of residence was possible only with notification to authorities. Authorities issue registered asylum seekers certificates that serve as identification documents and protect them from expulsion. In accordance with the law, they also must register with local authorities of their place of residence to obtain identity documents.

Temporary Protection: Although the government in the past provided temporary protection to individuals who may not qualify as refugees, it did not do so during the year.

Stateless Persons

As of January 1, 2012, the UNHCR listed 6,969 stateless persons in the country, of whom 6,559 had permanent residence, 292 held temporary residence permits valid up to three months, and 118 held temporary residence permits valid up to one year.

Permanently resident stateless persons held residence permits and were treated comparably to citizens in terms of access to employment, with the exception of a limited number of positions in the public sector that were available only to citizens. Stateless persons, however, faced de facto discrimination in employment, since authorities often required them to settle in rural areas where the range of employment opportunities was limited and prohibited them from seeking jobs outside of those regions. Stateless persons could not change their region of residence.

According to official statistics, approximately half of the stateless population resided in rural areas, i.e., areas that were outside the capital and the administrative centers of regions/oblasts and districts. According to a social survey of stateless persons conducted by the UNHCR office in 2011, approximately 17 percent of the stateless population were in Belarus before 1991 and became stateless after dissolution of the Soviet Union. Approximately 65 percent arrived in 1992-2000 and only 19 percent after 2001.

Section 3. Respect for Political Rights: The Right of Citizens to Change Their Government

The law provides the right for citizens to change their government peacefully, but the government consistently denied citizens this right.

Since his election in 1994 to a four-year term as the country's first president, Lukashenka steadily consolidated power in the executive branch to dominate all branches of government, effectively ending any separation of powers among the branches. Flawed referenda in 1996 and 2004 amended the constitution to broaden his powers, extend his term in office, and remove presidential term limits. Subsequent presidential elections, including the one held in 2010, continued to deny citizens the right to express their will to choose among opposing candidates in an honest and transparent process with fair access to independent media and resources.

Elections and Political Participation

Recent Elections: The 2010 presidential election was marred by numerous violations of procedures and an absence of transparency and accountability that led the Organization for Security and Cooperation in Europe's (OSCE) Office for Democratic Institutions and Human Rights (ODIHR) observer mission to report that the country still had "a considerable way to go in meeting its international commitments." OSCE/ODIHR observers assessed the vote count as "bad or very bad in almost half of all observed polling stations," with clear instances of ballot stuffing and tampering. Although opposition candidates enjoyed somewhat greater freedom to enter the race and promote their candidacies than in earlier elections, pre-election campaigning remained extremely limited, and government harassment of independent newspapers, opposition political parties, and independent NGOs throughout the year limited the opposition's ability to mount effective campaigns.

According to the OSCE/ODIHR mission, broadcasters nationwide devoted 90 percent of their political coverage to Lukashenka, and coverage of opposition candidates was overwhelmingly negative. Despite a nominal increase in opposition representation, authorities continued to exclude opposition representatives from election commissions at all levels. The majority of observers at local polling places appeared to be from government-sponsored NGOs. Many of them received instructions in advance to report to foreign observers that the proceedings were "in order" or to harass independent observers.

The most serious violations took place after the polls closed, when, as the OSCE/ODIHR mission observed, the situation "deteriorated significantly." In many instances international observers reported that counting was conducted silently and at a sufficient distance from observers, which prevented evaluation of the count. There were a number of reports that vote totals changed as the ballot boxes were transported between local precincts and the territorial election commission offices. Although no independent organizations were permitted to conduct exit polls, the NGO "For Fair Elections" stated that Lukashenka failed to gain the 50 percent of the vote necessary to avoid a runoff in the 250 polling stations it monitored. The official results gave him 79.65 percent of the vote against nine other candidates.

Elections in the lower house of the National Assembly took place in September 2012. The final report by the OSCE/ODIHR mission stated that the elections fell significantly short of international standards for democratic elections and that the same shortcomings encountered in the 2010 elections were repeated. The report stated that, despite some improvements to the electoral law, many OSCE commitments, including citizens' rights to associate, run as candidates, and express themselves freely, were not respected. The elections also were not administered in an impartial manner, especially regarding the composition of election commissions; an honest vote count could not be guaranteed; and the complaints and appeals process did not guarantee an effective remedy.

On December 8, several new amendments to the electoral code took effect. The amendments introduce a simple majority system in the first round of elections for the National Assembly. They also end the government practice of providing public funds for printing candidates' campaign materials while increasing the maximum size of private campaign funds. In addition the amendments prohibit citizens from campaigning to disrupt elections and referendums or to have them cancelled or postponed. Other changes include regulations on who can appeal for a vote recount and what type of questions can be put to a public referendum. Some members of the democratic opposition alleged that the amendments disproportionately targeted their candidates and activities.

Political Parties: Authorities routinely harassed and impeded the activities of opposition political parties and activists. Some opposition parties lacked legal status, since authorities refused to register them, and the government routinely interfered with the right to organize, run for election, seek votes, and publicize views. Approximately half a dozen largely inactive, but officially registered pro-Lukashenka political parties were allowed to operate freely, even though they appeared to be little more than fig leaves for a system that, de facto, excluded party politics.

The law allows authorities to suspend parties for six months after one warning and close them after two. During the year political parties did not receive any formal warnings, but members of parties that authorities refused to register, such as the Belarus Christian Democracy Party, continued to be subjected to harassment and arbitrary checks. The law also prohibits political parties from receiving support from abroad and requires all political groups and coalitions to register with the Ministry of Justice.

Authorities continued to harass the unrecognized Union of Poles of Belarus and its members.

<u>Participation of Women and Minorities</u>: There were no laws preventing women or minorities from voting or participating in political life on the same basis as men or nonminority citizens.

In the lower house of the National Assembly, women held 29 of the 109 seats. In the upper house, women held 20 of the 58 seats. A woman led one of the 24 government ministries. The National Bank and the Central Election Committee also were headed by women. Data on the participation of members of minorities in government was not available.

Section 4. Corruption and Lack of Transparency in Government

The law provides criminal penalties for official corruption, but reports indicated that officials continued to engage in corrupt practices. The World Bank's Worldwide Governance Indicators reflected that corruption was a serious problem in the country.

<u>Corruption</u>: According to official sources, most corruption cases involved soliciting and accepting bribes, fraud, and abuse of power, although anecdotal evidence indicated such corruption usually did not occur as part of day-to-day interaction between citizens and minor state officials.

The absence of an independent judicial system and law enforcement, the lack of separation of powers, and a harried independent press barred largely from interaction with a nontransparent state bureaucracy made it virtually impossible to gauge the scale of corruption or combat it effectively.

The Prosecutor General's Office is responsible for organizing and coordinating activities to combat corruption, including monitoring law enforcement operations, analyzing efficacy of implemented measures, supervising engaged parties, and drafting further legislation.

Authorities reported registering 1,779 corruption crimes during 2012, down 26.4 percent from 2011. Among these, bribery accounted for 933 cases, abuse of office or authority for 224 cases, and embezzlement through abuse of office for 546 cases. The number of persons convicted for these offenses declined 15 percent from 2011 to 1,151. The highest corruption rates were registered in the industrial, education, agricultural, health care, and construction sectors. According to prosecutors, the average bribe was $300, paid in U.S. currency, and the highest bribe was $500,000.

During 2012 officials of agencies responsible for maintaining state security, including financial intelligence, the Defense Ministry, and customs and border agencies, committed 116 corruption-related crimes, down from 252 crimes in 2010, or 4.8 percent of all corruption-related crimes. The Military Prosecutor's Office investigated and filed in court 11 cases of corruption and reimbursed more than 60 million rubles ($6,400) in damages resulting from corruption during the year.

There were numerous corruption prosecutions during the year, but prosecutions remained selective, nontransparent, and appeared in some cases politically motivated. For example, on March 25, a military panel of the Supreme Court sentenced Yauhen Poludzen, a former deputy minister of internal affairs, to three and a half years in prison and the forfeiture of his property for abuse of power.

Whistleblower Protection: There is no separate law that provides protection to public and private employees for making internal disclosures or lawful public disclosures of evidence of illegality. Separate provisions in the law on countering corruption, the criminal procedure code, and the law enforcement operations act outline protection measures for individuals who are party to an investigation or a criminal or civil case. A lack of transparency made it impossible to assess whether the law was implemented effectively.

Financial Disclosure: Anticorruption laws require income and asset disclosure by appointed and elected officials, their spouses, and members of households who have reached legal age and continue to live with them in the same household. According to the law, specialized anticorruption departments within the Prosecutor General's Office, the KGB, and the Interior Ministry monitor and verify anticorruption practices, and the prosecutor general and all other prosecutors are mandated to oversee the enforcement of anticorruption law. These declarations are not made available to the public. An exception applies to candidates running in presidential, parliamentary, and municipal elections. There are administrative sanctions and disciplinary penalties for noncompliance.

Public Access to Information: The law, government policies, and a presidential decree severely restricted public access to government information. Citizens had some access to certain categories of information on government databases and websites, but much of the information was neither current nor complete.

Section 5. Governmental Attitude Regarding International and Nongovernmental Investigation of Alleged Violations of Human Rights

There were a number of active domestic human rights NGOs, although authorities were often hostile to their efforts, did not cooperate with them, and were not responsive to their views.

Three prominent human rights NGOs – the BHC, the Center for Human Rights, and the Center for Legal Transformations – remained registered. The government refused to register numerous NGOs, thus placing them at risk under the criminal code, which criminalizes organizing or participating in any activity by an unregistered organization. The law also prohibits persons from acting on behalf of unregistered NGOs. A variety of unregistered NGOs, including Vyasna, the "Solidarity" Committee for the Protection of the Repressed, the Human Rights Alliance, Legal Assistance to the Population, and For Religious Freedom, continued to operate in spite of systematic harassment from authorities.

Authorities harassed both registered and unregistered NGOs, subjected them to frequent inspections and threats of deregistration, and reportedly monitored their correspondence and telephone conversations. Authorities harassed family members of NGO leaders and civil society activists. The government ignored reports issued by human rights NGOs and rarely met with them. State-run media did not report on human rights NGOs and their actions.

Authorities can close an NGO after issuing only one warning that it violated the law. The most common pretexts prompting a warning or closure were failure to obtain a legal address and technical discrepancies in application documents. The law allows authorities to close an NGO for accepting what it considered illegal forms of foreign assistance and permits the Ministry of Justice to participate in any NGO activity and to review all NGO documents. NGOs also must submit detailed reports annually to the ministry about their activities, office locations, officers, and total numbers of members.

A 2008 presidential order increased rent tenfold for most NGOs. Prior to the order NGOs paid one euro ($1.35) per square foot of office space, compared with 10 euros ($13.50) charged to commercial groups. While some groups, including youth sports groups, charity organizations, and children's arts centers, continued to pay rent at the reduced rate, independent NGOs were required to pay the higher rate. Some NGOs were forced to close or move because of the higher rents. In 2010 a senior state property committee member stated that to be eligible for discounted rent rates, an NGO must actively support government policies.

On April 1, the rent rate for the Francisak Skaryna Belarusian Language Society in Minsk rose by 60 percent after the Council of Ministers did not include the NGO on a list of groups entitled to low office rent rates.

In November 2012 the unregistered human rights NGO Vyasna was forced to abandon its office of 12 years, which was confiscated as part of the court sentence against its imprisoned leader, Ales Byalyatski. The group used Byalyatski's apartment as an office because it was not able to rent property without being registered. During the year the Belarusian Helsinki Committee's accounts remained blocked due to tax arrears and a complaint it sent to the United Nations regarding repression of lawyers. In 2008 the Supreme Court allowed the Ministry of Justice to withdraw a petition to suspend the BHC's activities. Nevertheless, at year's end the NGO's bank accounts remained blocked, and alleged tax arrears were unresolved.

The KGB continued to harass NGO and political party members and activists by planting defamatory articles or information about them in the media. For example, on June 2, Belarusian State Television Channel 1 aired a program entitled "System Virus," which alleged that civil society collaborated with Western donor countries to undermine the government.

Authorities were reluctant to engage on human rights problems with international NGOs and other human rights officials, and international NGO representatives often had difficulty gaining admission to the country.

Authorities routinely ignored local and international NGO recommendations on improving human rights in the country and requests to stop harassing the NGO community.

UN and Other International Bodies: In 2010 a Foreign Ministry spokesman announced that there were "no objective reasons" for extending the mandate of the OSCE office in Minsk, despite the fact that the mandate of the office had not been fulfilled. The government claimed that the OSCE mandate "has been fulfilled" and pointed to the earlier closure of OSCE missions in neighboring countries. On October 17, a Ministry of Foreign Affairs spokesperson stated that the government was not considering the possibility of reopening the Minsk OSCE office.

In June the UN Human Rights Council extended the mandate of Miklos Haraszti as the special rapporteur on the human rights situation in Belarus. During the year Haraszti released two reports on the situation of human rights in the country. Authorities stated that they would refuse any cooperation with the special rapporteur's mission, and consequently he was not permitted to travel to the country.

Government Human Rights Bodies: A standing commission on human rights in the lower chamber of parliament was ineffective.

Section 6. Discrimination, Societal Abuses, and Trafficking in Persons

The law prohibits discrimination based on race, gender, language, or social status, but the government did not always enforce these prohibitions.

Women

Rape and Domestic Violence: The law criminalizes rape in general but does not include separate provisions on marital rape. Rape was a problem, but most women did not report it due to shame or fear that police would blame the victim. According to the Ministry of Internal Affairs, there were 68 registered cases of rape from January to September 2012, down 32.7 percent compared with the same period in 2011.

Domestic violence was a significant problem. In 2011 the Office of the UN High Commissioner for Human Rights raised grave concerns about the persistence of violence against women, in particular domestic and sexual violence, its underreporting, the lack of prosecution of violence within the family, the fact that rape was subject to private rather than official prosecution, and the lack of shelters for victims of domestic violence. State-run district centers for social services across the country ran 47 crisis rooms for victims, including domestic violence victims, and two more shelters for victims of domestic violence located at a monastery and run by an NGO.

The criminal code does not contain a separate article dealing with domestic violence. According to a study released by the Belarus State University's Center for Sociological and Political Research in 2010, four out of five women between the ages of 18 and 60 claimed they were subjected to psychological violence in their families. One in four women suffered from physical violence, and 13 percent of women reported their partners sexually abused them. Women remained reluctant to report domestic violence due to fear of reprisal and social stigma and due to fear that if the aggressor were fined, the financial burden would fall on the family. According to the study, only 6 percent of male and 46 percent of female victims of domestic violence sought professional assistance. NGOs operated crisis shelters, primarily in Minsk, but they were poorly funded and received only limited support from the government. Government efforts to combat gender-based violence were mainly directed at preventing such crimes and not at protecting or assisting victims, although crisis rooms provided limited psychological and medical assistance to victims. Authorities did not tackle the root causes of violence, including alcoholism, social stigma, and gender-based stereotypes.

From January through October 2012, authorities registered 1,502 domestic crimes, including 88 cases of premeditated murder, 219 cases of deliberately inflicting grave bodily injury, and 234 cases of torture.

Sexual Harassment: Sexual harassment reportedly was widespread, but no specific laws, other than those against physical assault, address the problem.

Reproductive Rights: Couples and individuals have the right to decide the number, spacing, and timing of children, and had the information and means to do so free from discrimination. Access to information on contraception and skilled attendance at delivery and in postpartum care were widely available.

Discrimination: The law provides for equal treatment of women with regard to property ownership and inheritance, family law, and the judicial system, and the law was generally respected. The law also requires equal wages for equal work, although this provision was not always enforced.

The National Statistics Committee reported that, as of December 2012, a total of 48.2 percent of unemployed persons were women, compared with 62.8 percent in December 2011. The committee also noted that on average men found new employment in one month, while women searched for more than two months. Women also accounted for two-thirds of all officially unemployed persons seeking a job for more than a year.

Very few women were in the upper ranks of management or government, and most women were concentrated in the lower-paid public sector. Women's groups also voiced concerns about the feminization of poverty, particularly among women with more than two children, female-headed households, women taking care of family members with disabilities or older family members, rural women, and older women.

Although the law grants women the right to three years of maternity leave with assurance of job availability upon return, employers often circumvented employment protections by using short-term contracts, then refusing to renew a woman's contract when she became pregnant. A number of women worked in extreme and hazardous conditions.

Children

Birth Registration: Citizenship is derived either by birth within the country's territory or from one's parents. A child of a citizen is a citizen regardless of place of birth, even if one of the parents is not a citizen. In general births were registered immediately.

Education: There continued to be isolated reports that non-Romani children and teachers subjected Romani children to harassment. The majority of Romani youth did not finish secondary school and failed to enroll in university programs, although the situation improved as more Romani children from mixed families enrolled and obtained bachelor degrees, including in the regions. There were no special school programs for Roma, although there were such programs for Jews, ethnic Lithuanians, and Poles.

<u>Child Abuse</u>: Rape or sexual assault of a person known to be a minor is punishable by up to 15 years in jail. Sexual acts between a person older than 18 years of age and a person known to be younger than age 16 carry penalties of up to five years in jail. According to NGOs that assist child abuse victims, authorities reported approximately 238 criminal cases during 2012 in which children were victims of various forms of sexual abuse and molestation, including rape. The Education Ministry reported on emotional and physical abuse against children that did not require forensic investigations. According to the most recent statistics available, in 2006 approximately 10 percent of children between the ages of 10 and 17 were victims of psychological abuse in their families, and 4.5 percent were victims of physical abuse.

<u>Forced and Early Marriage</u>: The legal minimum age of marriage for both boys and girls is 18, although girls as young as 14 can be married legally with parental consent. There were reports of early marriage in which girls as young as 14 and boys as young as 16 were married with parental consent. The government registered 904 marriages involving children in 2011, up from 856 in 2010. In the majority of these cases, children were married with parental consent.

<u>Sexual Exploitation of Children</u>: The minimum age of consensual sex is 16. Prostitution of children was a problem. According to data from the Ministry of Internal Affairs, 44 minors became victims of trafficking-related crimes for sexual exploitation in the January to September 2012 period. The law provides penalties of up to 13 years in jail for production or distribution of pornographic materials depicting a minor. The law generally was enforced. In 2012 the Ministry of Internal Affairs reportedly registered 40 criminal cases in connection with the production and distribution of child pornography, including 34 cases of distribution on the internet during the year.

<u>Institutionalized Children</u>: There was no system for monitoring child abuse in orphanages or other specialized institutions. Authorities did not report on any child abuse incidents. During the year there were reports of alleged abuse in foster families. The government opened investigations into some of these cases.

In 2007-08 the Education Ministry and the UN Children's Fund conducted a national survey to assess child abuse in the country. According to the ministry, 20 percent of institutionalized children ages 10 to 17 reported psychological abuse by family members, and 22 percent reported that they were victims of physical abuse. Independent observers suggested that the numbers were likely higher, since approximately 30 percent of children refused to answer this question.

International Child Abductions: The country is a party to the 1980 Hague Convention on the Civil Aspects of International Child Abduction.

Anti-Semitism

Jewish groups estimated that between 30,000 and 40,000 persons identified themselves as Jews. Most were not active religiously.

Anti-Semitic incidents continued but were on the decline, and authorities sporadically investigated reports of such acts. Religious sites were vandalized. On October 29, three underage vandals damaged a monument commemorating local residents and Jews killed by the Nazis in 1942 in the village of Kuranets; the vandals also destroyed the surrounding fence. Although police detained and interrogated the three minors, they were not held liable due to their age, although their names were entered into police records.

The government did not promote antibias and tolerance education. Jewish community and civil society activists expressed concern over the concept of a "greater Slavic union" that was popular among nationalist organizations, including the neo-Nazi group Russian National Unity, which remained active despite its official dissolution in 2000. Neo-Nazis were widely believed to be behind anti-Semitic incidents across the country. Anti-Semitic and Russian ultranationalist newspapers, literature, DVDs, and videotapes imported from Russia were sold.

Trafficking in Persons

See the Department of State's *Trafficking in Persons Report* at www.state.gov/j/tip/.

Persons with Disabilities

The law does not specifically prohibit discrimination against persons with physical, sensory, intellectual, or mental disabilities in employment, education, air travel and other transportation, access to health care, and other government services, and discrimination was common.

The Ministry of Labor and Social Security is the main government agency responsible for protecting the rights of persons with disabilities, who accounted for more than half a million persons. The law mandates that transport, residences, and businesses be accessible to persons with disabilities, but few public areas were wheelchair accessible. The National Association of Disabled Wheelchair Users estimated that more than 90 percent of persons with physical disabilities were unable to leave their places of residence without assistance, and their places of residence were not built to accommodate wheelchair users. While authorities claimed that 30 percent of the country's total infrastructure was accessible, disability rights organizations disputed this figure.

A government prohibition against workdays longer than seven hours for persons with disabilities reportedly made companies reluctant to hire them. Local NGOs reported that 80 percent of persons with disabilities were unemployed. Authorities provided minimal welfare benefits for persons with disabilities, and calculations of pensions did not take disability status into account. Members of the country's paralympic teams received half the salaries and prize money of athletes without disabilities.

The country's lack of independent living opportunities left many persons with disabilities no choice but to live in state-run institutions. Approximately 70 such institutions existed across the country. Disability rights organizations reported that the quality of care in these facilities was low, and instances of mistreatment and abuse were reported. Persons with physical disabilities and persons with mental disabilities frequently were mixed within facilities and not provided specialized care. Public transportation was free to persons with disabilities, but neither the subway in Minsk nor the bus system was wheelchair accessible. According to government statistics, 2 percent of the country's public transportation network was accessible.

Disability rights organizations reported difficulty organizing advocacy activities due to impediments to freedom of assembly, censorship of materials, and the government's unwillingness to register assistance projects.

Advocates also noted that persons with disabilities, especially those who were visually and hearing impaired, lacked the ability to address violations of their rights easily and completely since courts often failed to provide special equipment and sign language translation.

National/Racial/Ethnic Minorities

Governmental and societal discrimination against ethnic Poles and Roma persisted. There were also expressions of societal hostility toward proponents of Belarusian national culture, which the government often identified with actors of the democratic opposition, repeatedly labeled by Lukashenka as "the fifth column."

Authorities continued to harass the independent and unregistered Union of Poles of Belarus.

Official and societal discrimination continued against the country's 10,000 to 20,000 Roma. The Romani community continued to experience high unemployment and low levels of education. Authorities estimated the unemployment rate among Roma to be as high as 80 percent, according to the latest available information. Roma often were denied access to higher education in state-run universities. In general Roma hold Belarusian citizenship but many lacked official government identity documents.

In August local authorities in Zhlobin demolished seven houses in a local Romani community without providing alternative housing for the Roma living there. The forcible eviction took place during preparations for the annual Dazhynki harvest festival, and authorities did not provide any financial compensation to the residents. The deputy head of the district executive committee refused to comment on the evictions.

While the Russian and Belarusian languages have equal legal status, Russian was the primary language used by the government. According to independent polling, the overwhelming majority of the population spoke Russian as its mother tongue. Because the government viewed many proponents of the Belarusian language as political opponents of the regime, authorities continued to harass and intimidate academic and cultural groups that sought to promote use of the Belarusian language and routinely rejected proposals to widen use of the language.

Societal Abuses, Discrimination, and Acts of Violence Based on Sexual Orientation and Gender Identity

Consensual same-sex sexual conduct is not illegal, but discrimination against LGBT persons was widespread, and harassment occurred.

Authorities routinely denied LGBT groups permission to hold public events, including a pride parade. The Minsk City Executive Committee denied permission for the LGBT community to hold public demonstrations in the city on December 11 and 12. Authorities also blocked the opening of Minsk Gay Pride 2013 on December 6. Organizers of Gay Pride 2013 cancelled all LGBT events and parties scheduled for December 7, allegedly because of government pressure. For example, the Minsk restaurant "Casa Augstin Lopez" cancelled a December 7 event because of "a broken sewer pipe," while police blocked people from entering another LGBT-friendly club the same evening. In addition police came to a Belarusian Free Theater performance dedicated to the event to "check on a report that people having a non-traditional sexual orientation gather at the address."

Throughout the year police raided LGBT clubs across the country, interviewed LGBT activists about their activities, and in several cases briefly detained LGBT individuals without charge. For example, on January 11 and 12, police raided LGBT clubs in Minsk and Vitsyebsk. Police recorded the passport information and questioned those present. On January 14 and 15, police summoned Lambda members to police stations in Brest, Baranavichy, Mahilyow, Minsk, and Vitsyebsk and interviewed them about their activities and the organization's leader, Syarhey Androsenka.

In February police detained LGBT activist Ihar Tsikhanyuk while he was undergoing treatment at a hospital. Police officers reportedly punched and insulted him, taunted him for being gay, and threatened him with more violence. After the police officers returned him to the hospital, hospital staff reportedly refused to document his injuries.

On April 18, the Supreme Court rejected an appeal against the Justice Ministry's decision to deny official registration to Lambda.

In August authorities forced the closure of the Minsk and regional offices of "Vstrecha," an organization that focuses on HIV/AIDS education and support for men who have sex with men. Twice during the year, authorities summoned the organization's coordinator, Vadzim Kruk, for interrogation on the organization's activities, information about other LGBT activists, and his personal life. During the year the Vityebsk regional coordinator for the organization was asked to vacate his office because other NGOs that shared the office space faced government pressure for associating with LGBT-affiliated organizations. The organization maintained its official registration at year's end.

On December 7, police raided a flat rented by several persons participating in LGBT pride events. The police copied the passport data of the nine persons who were present and then demanded that they leave the apartment or face possible arrest.

Societal discrimination against LGBT activists persisted, with the tacit support of the regime.

In March Lukashenka stated that he could not "forgive" homosexuality in men, and in April he stated, "We should not be forced to introduce same-sex marriages. This will not happen in the near future. That is for sure, when I am the president." In July Lukashenka condemned same-sex marriages as a "tragic sin of a general spiritual crisis and the Western world's blindness."

Other Societal Violence or Discrimination

Societal discrimination against persons with HIV/AIDS remained a problem, and the illness carried a heavy stigma. The Joint UN Program on HIV/AIDS office reported that there were numerous reports of HIV-infected individuals who faced discrimination, especially at workplaces and during job interviews.

According to a 2011 study by the UN Fund for Population Activities, 31 percent of surveyed doctors indicated their reluctance to work with HIV-positive persons. Only 8 percent expressed a positive attitude towards HIV-infected patients. More than 16 percent of doctors reported that they lacked knowledge for treating such patients efficiently.

A number of NGOs representing HIV-infected persons continued to express serious concerns about a 2011 law aimed at preventing the spread of the virus and other dangerous and primarily communicable diseases. According to a UN Development Program expert, the law risks stigmatizing HIV-infected persons and forcing them "underground." The law extends the list of grounds for mandatory HIV testing and requires HIV-positive persons to inform all their former partners of their status. According to rights advocates, the law risks further stigmatizing not only HIV-infected persons but also their families, breaching their privacy and medical secrecy, and turning them away from state-run medical and social institutions.

Although the government adopted a national program for combating HIV in 2011-15, which for the first time prescribes funds to procure imported antiretroviral treatment for HIV-infected persons, a near three-fold devaluation of the country's currency in 2011 significantly reduced the effective purchasing power of the resources committed to this effort. The government continued to broadcast and post public service advertisements raising awareness about HIV/AIDS and calling for greater tolerance toward persons infected with the virus.

There were also frequent reports of family discrimination against HIV-positive members of households. This included preventing HIV-positive parents from seeing their children or requiring HIV-positive family members to use separate dishware.

Section 7. Worker Rights

a. Freedom of Association and the Right to Collective Bargaining

Although the law protects the rights of workers, except state security and military personnel, to form and join independent unions and to strike, it places a number of serious restrictions on the exercise of these rights. The law provides for the right to organize and bargain collectively but does not protect against antiunion discrimination.

The government barely tolerated independent unions. The government-controlled Federation of Trade Unions of Belarus is the largest union, claiming more than four million members, although that number likely was inflated, since the country's total workforce was approximately four million. It largely resembles its Soviet predecessors and serves as a control mechanism and distributor of benefits. The Belarusian Congress of Democratic Trade Unions (BCDTU), with four constituent unions and approximately 10,000 members of independent trade unions, is the largest independent union umbrella organization, but tight government control over registration requirements and public demonstrations made it difficult for the federation to organize and strike.

Prohibitive registration requirements that any new independent union have a large membership and cooperation from the employer presented significant obstacles to union formation. State control reportedly increased as a result of the continuing economic difficulties, and authorities fiercely resisted attempts by workers to leave the official union and join the independent one.

Management and local authorities blocked worker attempts to organize strikes on many occasions by declaring them illegal. The legal requirements to conduct a strike are high. For example, strikes can only be held at least three months after dispute settlement between the union and employer has failed. In addition a minimum number of workers must continue to work during the strike. Nevertheless, these requirements were largely irrelevant, since the unions that represented almost all workers were under government control. Government authorities and managers of state-owned enterprises routinely interfered with union activities and hindered workers' efforts to bargain collectively, in some instances arbitrarily suspending collective bargaining agreements. Union members who participated in public demonstrations were subject to arrest and detention. Due to a persistent atmosphere of repression and the fear of imprisonment, in general few public demonstrations took place during the year.

The International Trade Union Confederation's *Annual Survey of Violations of Trade Union Rights* for 2012 noted that in 2011 authorities adopted amendments to the Law on Mass Activities that seriously limited demonstrations, rallies, and other public action, constraining the right of unions to organize and strike. In November 2012 the International Labor Organization's (ILO) Committee on Application and Standards noted that the government did not undertake any response to ILO requests to take measures to amend the presidential decree which creates obstacles to trade union registration and operations.

The government continued efforts to suppress independent unions, stop union activities, and bring all union activity fully under its control. Its efforts included frequent refusals to extend employment contracts for members of independent unions and refusals to register independent unions. According to BCDTU leader Alyaksandr Yarashuk, no independent unions have been established since a 1999 decree requiring trade unions to register with the government. Workers who were deemed "natural leaders" or who involved themselves in NGOs or opposition political activities were routinely fired for these activities.

For example, in April the management of the state-owned mining company Hranit in the town of Mikashevichy denied any political motivation behind the dismissal of Anatol Litvinka, a member of the grassroots Belarusian Independent Trade Union (BITU).

One month later, Hranit did not prolong the contract of Leanid Dubanosau, another member of the BITU. Litvinka and Dubanosau are the seventh and eighth members of the independent trade union to be dismissed from Hranit. Aleh Stakhayevich, chairman of the local trade union chapter, condemned the dismissal and stated that Dubanosau was the last Hranit employee who paid official BITU membership dues.

Additionally, local authorities continued to deny multiple registration applications by the Vitsyebsk, Mahilyow, and Homyel chapters of the REP. On August 5, local authorities in Borisov revoked the registration of the local REP organization, which had been officially registered since 2007. The IndustriALL Global Union demanded that the local authorities immediately reverse this decision.

Authorities and state-run enterprises continued to pressure independent trade unions and deny their right to sign collective bargaining agreements.

The government requires state employees, who constitute approximately 80 percent of the workforce, to sign short-term work contracts. Although such contracts may have terms of up to five years, most expired after one year, which gave the government the ability to fire employees by declining to renew their contracts. Many members of independent unions, political parties, and civil society groups lost their jobs because of this practice. A government edict provides the possibility for employers to sign open-ended work contracts after five years of good conduct. The edict limits the right of employers to approve open-ended contracts earlier than five years after the service computation date. The provision does not apply to state employees and other categories of workers who remained subject to mandatory contracts.

For example, in June the hospital administration in Slonim did not prolong the contract of Ivan Sheha, a medical doctor and member of the Belarusian Popular Front. Alyaksei Yanukevich, chairman of the Belarusian Popular Front, condemned the decision as politically motivated. The Ministry of Health denied any political motivation. Sheha continued to see patients free of charge at his home.

b. Prohibition of Forced or Compulsory Labor

The law prohibits all forms of forced or compulsory labor, but the government did not effectively enforce its provisions.

During the year the government approved "subbotniks," which require employees of the government, state enterprises, and many private businesses to work on Saturday and donate their earnings to finance government social and other projects. For example, the construction of the Great Patriotic War Museum was accomplished by use of subbotniks. On March 19, authorities reported that approximately 70,000 people participated in a subbotnik to clean Minsk streets following a snowstorm. On April 20, authorities reported that more than three and a half million people participated in a subbotnik, cleaning streets or performing their regular work duties across the country. Employers and authorities intimidated and fined workers who refused to participate.

There were reports that authorities forced military conscripts to perform work that was unrelated to their military service. Credible sources also reported labor practices amounting to forced labor in prisons. Former inmates stated that their monthly wages were as low as 5,000 rubles ($0.54). Authorities also continued to employ unpaid agricultural labor and sent university and high school students to help farmers during the harvesting season.

On April 19, Lukashenka defended a December 2012 decree that prohibits workers in state-run wood processing factories and associated companies from quitting their jobs without prior permission from their managers during the implementation of state-subsidized upgrades of factories. The decree obliges factories and subcontractors, which employed approximately 18,000 persons, to pay monthly allowances to their workers in addition to their regular salaries, which workers would be forced to pay back if they quit their job without management approval or were fired. If workers have no means to repay or are unemployed, they would be forced to return to their previous workplaces and repay allowances from their regular salaries. In addition all subcontractors would be charged and fined if they failed to implement their projects on time. An employee who disagreed with the employer's decision could appeal directly to the governor of the region, but the decree does not specify how governors should act on such appeals.

In November the management of Babruysk-based AAT Fandok refused to accept the resignation of worker Natalya Ivanova, citing Lukashenka's December 2012 decree. Ivanova wrote that she wanted to leave the company because she had leg problems. Although Ivanova's employment contract expired on November 26, Fandok director general Uladzimir Radzyukevich ordered the contract to be prolonged until 2015 unless the woman provided written confirmation that she could not work at the plywood plant for health reasons. Only if she submitted a sickness certificate would she be released from the obligation to pay more than three million rubles ($320) to Fandok under the decree. Ivanova sent a complaint to the head of the Mahilyow Regional Executive Committee but as of year's end had not received a reply.

Also see the Department of State's *Trafficking in Persons Report* at www.state.gov/j/tip/.

c. Prohibition of Child Labor and Minimum Age for Employment

The minimum age for employment is 16, but children as young as 14 may conclude a labor contract with the written consent of one parent or a legal guardian. The Prosecutor General's Office reportedly enforced the law effectively. Minors under the age of 18 are allowed to work in nonhazardous jobs but are not allowed to work overtime, on weekends, or on government holidays. Work may not be harmful to children's health or hinder their education.

The government generally enforced these laws; nevertheless, there were reports that some children were forced to work. For example, in some localities schoolchildren were induced to help local collective farms with the harvest in September and October.

d. Acceptable Conditions of Work

As of December 2012 the national minimum monthly wage was 1,171,610 rubles ($125). As of December 2012 the average monthly wage was 4,244,270 rubles ($453). As of November 2012 the government set the poverty line at 880,030 rubles ($94) a month per capita.

The law establishes a standard workweek of 40 hours and provides for at least one 24-hour rest period per week. Because of the country's difficult economic situation, many workers worked considerably fewer than 40 hours per week, and factories often required workers to take unpaid furloughs due to lack of demand for the factories' products. The law permits furloughs only with the consent of the employee. The law provides for mandatory overtime and holiday pay and restricts overtime to 10 hours a week, with a maximum of 180 hours of overtime each year.

The law establishes minimum conditions for workplace safety and worker health, but employers often ignored these standards. Workers at many heavy machinery plants did not wear minimal safety gear. The state labor inspectorate lacked authority to enforce employer compliance and often ignored violations. The government reported that approximately 400,000 persons worked in the informal economy. Informal workers were not covered by legal workplace standards.

As of December 2012 the Ministry of Labor and Social Security reported 163 workplace fatalities, down from 186 during the same period in 2011. The ministry reported that the majority of workplace accidents occurred in the construction industry and were caused by carelessness, poor conditions, malfunctioning equipment, and poor training and instruction. The law does not provide workers the right to remove themselves from dangerous and unhealthy work environments without risking loss of employment.

www.ingramcontent.com/pod-product-compliance
Lightning Source LLC
Chambersburg PA
CBHW080613290526
45790CB00007B/2764